To: Marshall~

Your mission is to
read _even_ _more_!

[signature]

2.16

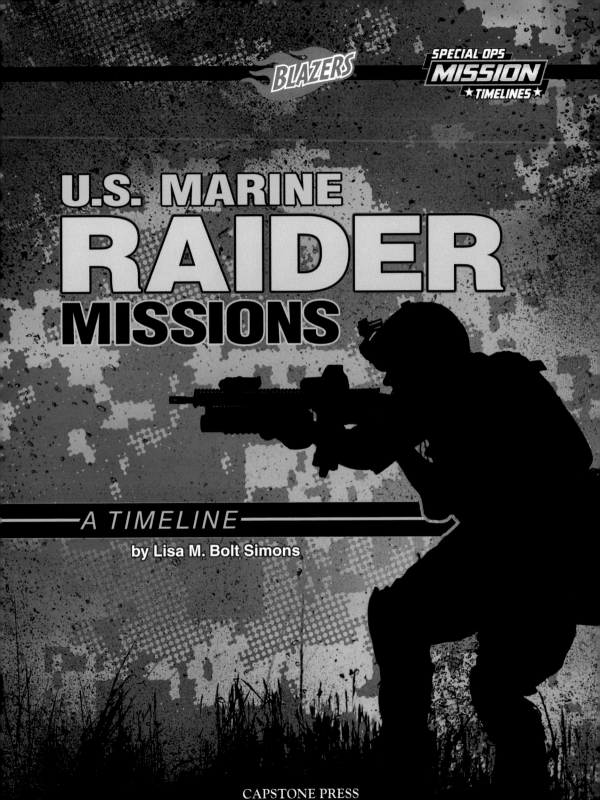

BLAZERS

SPECIAL OPS
MISSION
★ TIMELINES ★

U.S. MARINE RAIDER MISSIONS

A TIMELINE

by Lisa M. Bolt Simons

CAPSTONE PRESS
a capstone imprint

Blazers Books are published by Capstone Press,
1710 Roe Crest Drive, North Mankato, Minnesota 56003
www.mycapstone.com

Library of Congress Cataloging-in-Publication Data
Simons, Lisa M. B., 1969– author.
U.S. Marine raider missions : a timeline / by Lisa M. Bolt Simons.
pages cm.—(Blazers. Special Ops mission timelines)
Includes bibliographical references and index.
Summary: "Introduces readers to major special operation missions of the U.S. Marine Corps
in a timeline format"—Provided by publisher.
Audience: Grade 4 to 6.
ISBN 978-1-4914-8704-4 (library binding)
ISBN 978-1-4914-8708-2 (eBook PDF)
1. United States. Marine Special Operations Command—Juvenile literature. I. Title. II. Title:
United States Marine raider missions.
VE23.S56 2016
359.9'84—dc23   2015026239

Editorial Credits
Aaron Sautter, editor; Kyle Grenz, designer; Jo Miller, media researcher;
Lori Barbeau, production specialist

Capstone Press would like to thank Michael Doidge, Military Historian, for his assistance in
creating this book.

Photo Credits
AP Images, 21; Bridgeman Images: Private Collection/Peter Newark Historical Pictures/U.S.
Marines Capture the Barbary pirate fortress at Derna, Tripoli, 27th April 1805 (w/c on
paper), Waterhouse, C.H. (fl.1812), 7; Corbis: Don Troiani, 9; Getty Images: Archive Photos/
Buyenlarge, 11, John Cantlie, 27, Keystone, 15; Newscom: Everett Collection, 13, 19, REX/
Brian L Wickliffe, 28; Shutterstock: kanin.studio, Cover (silhouette), Karyl Miller, Cover (top
inset); U.S. Marine Corps photo by Cpl. Brian Reimers, 25, Cpl. Kyle McNally, Cover (bottom
inset), Lance Cpl. Stephen Benson, 29, Lance Cpl. Thomas W. Provost, 5, Sgt. Devin Nichols,
4, Wikimedia, 17, Wikimedia/USMC Photo A184966, 23

Design Elements
Getty Images: Photodisc; Shutterstock: ALMAGAMI

Printed in China by Nordica
1015/CA21501403
092015   009210S16

TABLE OF CONTENTS

New and Proud

The Marine Corps Forces Special Operations Command (MARSOC) was created in 2006. Marine special forces troops often carry out **amphibious** missions. They have been involved in such missions since the 1700s.

amphibious—describes a military action involving forces landing and attacking from the sea

SPECIAL FORCES
ARCHIVES
★★★★★

The Marine Corps Forces Special Operations teams were officially renamed Marine Raiders in 2015.

Battle of Derna

April 27, 1805

The First Barbary War (1801–1805) was fought to stop pirates in northern Africa. In 1805 eight Marines led a **mercenary** army 600 miles (966 kilometers) across the desert. Then they fought an eight-hour battle to capture the city of Derna, Tripoli.

mercenary—a soldier who is paid to fight for a foreign army

Battle of Derna

First Barbary War

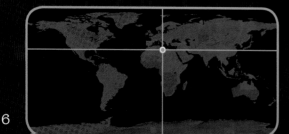

April 27, 1805

Location:
Derna, Tripoli
(present-day Libya)

Mission goal:
capture the second-largest city in Tripoli

Mission outcome:
enemy forces defeated, city captured

The Marine Corps was first formed on November 10, 1775, by the Continental Congress.

∧ The battle at Derna was the first land victory for U.S. forces overseas.

Battle of Baltimore

September 12–13, 1814

During the War of 1812 (1812–1815), British forces **bombarded** Fort McHenry in Baltimore, Maryland. Hundreds of Marines and sailors helped defend the city and fort. Baltimore and Fort McHenry stood strong. The British withdrew the next day.

bombard—to attack a place with heavy gunfire

CONFLICT:
AT A GLANCE

Battle of
Baltimore

War of 1812

September 12–13, 1814

Location:
Baltimore,
Maryland

Mission goal:
defend Fort McHenry

Mission outcome:
British attack defeated

SPECIAL FORCES ARCHIVES ★★★★★

Commodore John Rodgers commanded the Marines at the Battle of Baltimore. The position they defended became known as "Rodgers' Bastion."

| 1800 | 1900 | 2000 |

Battle of Derna

Battle of Drewry's Bluff

May 15, 1862

In the U.S. Civil War (1861–1865), the Union wanted to capture the **Confederate** capital of Richmond, Virginia. In 1862 Union Marines attacked Confederate forces on Drewry's Bluff near Richmond. But the Union troops had to withdraw when they ran out of ammunition.

Confederate—having to do with the Confederacy during the Civil War

CONFLICT:
AT A GLANCE

Battle of Drewry's Bluff

U.S. Civil War

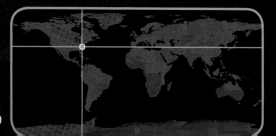

May 15, 1862

Location:
Richmond,
Virginia

Mission goal:
capture the
Confederate capital

Mission outcome:
Union Marines forced
to withdraw

Corporal John F. Mackie was awarded one of the first Medals of Honor in 1863 for his bravery at Drewry's Bluff. The medal was a first for a member of the Marine Corps.

∧ The Confederate's Fort Darling at Drewry's Bluff overlooked the river near Richmond, Virginia.

Battle in Belleau Wood

June 6–26, 1918

During World War I (1914–1918), Germany wanted to capture Paris, France. In 1918 a Marine **brigade** battled German forces at Belleau Wood near Paris. The Marines fought the Germans for 20 days. They kept the enemy out of the city.

brigade—a unit of an army, usually made up of two or more battalions

Battle in Belleau Wood

World War I

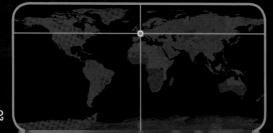

June 6–26, 1918

Location:
Belleau Wood, France

Mission goal:
stop the advance of German forces

Mission outcome:
German forces kept out of Paris

The Marine Corps had more than 1,000 **casualties** at Belleau Wood on June 6, 1918. It was the most casualties suffered since the Marines were formed in 1775.

∧ The battle at Belleau Wood, France was one of the largest and deadliest of World War I.

casualty—people who are injured, captured, killed, or missing in a battle or war

Operation Watchtower

August 7, 1942–February 9, 1943

Japan controlled many islands during World War II (1939–1945). In 1942 the Marines invaded Guadalcanal and other nearby islands. They captured an important airfield. After several months of fighting, Japanese forces retreated from the islands.

CONFLICT:
AT A GLANCE

Operation **Watchtower** **World War II**

August 7,1942–February 9,1943

Location:
Guadalcanal,
Solomon Islands

Mission goal:
capture Guadalcanal
and its airfield

Mission outcome:
Japan forced to retreat

In 1942 Navajo Indians were recruited as Marines. They became "Code Talkers." They used their native language to keep military secrets from the enemy.

⋀ The U.S. invasion of Guadalcanal was part of the first major attack against Japan's forces in World War II.

Operation Overlord

June 6, 1944

U.S. Marines had an important mission in the **D-Day** invasion of Europe. Marine riflemen stood at the top of the **Allies'** ships crossing the English Channel. They shot and blew up enemy mines in the water. The Marines helped the ships safely reach the beaches of Normandy, France.

D-Day—June 6, 1944, the day that thousands of Allied forces began their invasion of France to free the country and the rest of Europe from the Germans during World War II

Allies—a group of countries united against Germany during World War II, including France, the United States, Canada, Great Britain, and others

CONFLICT: *AT A GLANCE*

Operation Overlord

World War II

June 6, 1944

Location: English Channel

Mission goal: destroy enemy ocean mines

Mission outcome: Allied ships arrived safely at beaches in Normandy

Operation Detachment

February 19–March 26, 1945

The Marines fought hard to capture the island of Iwo Jima in 1945. Its airfields were important for U.S. forces. Enemy Japanese soldiers were protected inside **bunkers** and miles of tunnels. The Marines used flamethrowers to clear out the bunkers.

bunker—an underground shelter from bomb attacks and gunfire

CONFLICT: AT A GLANCE

Operation Detachment

World War II

February 19–March 26, 1945

Location: Iwo Jima, Japan

Mission goal: capture the island and its airfields

Mission outcome: Japanese forces defeated; captured important airfields

V The Marines also used flamethrowing tanks against enemy forces on Iwo Jima.

SPECIAL FORCES
ARCHIVES
★★★★★

The Imperial Japanese Army had dug 11 miles (17.7 km) of tunnels on the small island of Iwo Jima.

Battle of the Pusan Perimeter

July 31–September 16, 1950

In the Korean War (1950–1953), U.S. Marines helped defend the **perimeter** around Pusan, South Korea. They used air strikes, tanks, grenades, and **mortars** to fight North Korean forces. The enemy was finally forced to retreat.

perimeter—the outer edge or boundary of an area

mortar—a short cannon that fires shells or rockets high in the air

CONFLICT:
AT A GLANCE

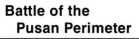

Battle of the
Pusan Perimeter

Korean War

July 31–September 16, 1950

Location:
Pusan,
South Korea

Mission goal:
protect Pusan and
its harbor

Mission outcome:
North Korea forced
to retreat

SPECIAL FORCES ARCHIVES
★ ★ ★ ★ ★

Marines used new M-26 Pershing tanks during the Korean War. The tanks carried three machine guns and traveled 30 miles (48 km) per hour.

Operation Starlite

August 18–24, 1965

During the Vietnam War (1959–1975), **Viet Cong** (VC) forces were discovered near an important military base in 1965. The Marines were sent by helicopter and boat to surround the enemy. It was the first U.S. victory against a large VC force.

Viet Cong—South Vietnamese rebel fighters who were aided by North Vietnam during the Vietnam War

CONFLICT: *AT A GLANCE*

Operation Starlite   **Vietnam War**

August 18–24, 1965

Location:
Quang Ngai province, Vietnam

Mission goal:
prevent an attack by the Viet Cong

Mission outcome:
trapped and defeated the enemy

The Marines used helicopters and tanks to carry wounded troops to safety.

USMC 201901

MARIN

1800
Battle of Derna   Battle of
                    Baltimore

Battle of
Drewry's Bluff

1900
Battle in
Belleau Wood

Operation
Watchtower

Operation
Overlord

Operation
Detachment

Battle of the
Pusan Perimeter

2000

23

Objective Razor

May–June 2004

Detachment One was a special Marine unit during the Iraq War (2003-2011). In one 2004 mission, the unit had to find an important enemy leader. The Marines used **intelligence** and **stealth** to track him down and capture him.

intelligence—secret information about an enemy's plans or actions

stealth—the ability to move without being detected

CONFLICT:
AT A GLANCE

Objective
Razor

Iraq War

May–June 2004

Location:
Baghdad, Iraq

Mission goal:
capture an important
enemy leader

Mission outcome:
target captured,
important information
obtained

Corporal Jason Dunham was the first Marine to receive a Medal of Honor in the Iraq War. On April 14, 2004, he jumped on a live grenade to save other Marines. He died a few days later from his injuries.

∧ The Marines raided many suspected enemy locations during the Iraq War.

1800   1900   2000

Afghanistan Ambush

June 14–16, 2012

In 2012 a small team of Marines was helping a village in Afghanistan. Enemy forces **ambushed** them. Two Marines were seriously wounded. The others risked their lives to rescue their teammates. The battle lasted for two days until the enemy was defeated.

ambush—to hide and make a surprise attack

∧ U.S. Marines had to always be ready for surprise attacks while on duty in Afghanistan.

1800
Battle of Derna

Battle of
Baltimore

Battle of
Drewry's Bluff

1900
Battle in
Belleau Wood

Operation
Watchtower

Operation
Overlord

Operation
Detachment

Battle of the
Pusan Perimeter

Operation
Starlite

2000
Objective
Razor

Protecting the World

The Marine Raiders' motto is "Always Faithful, Always Forward." Their mission is to help protect innocent people around the world. Forty-eight special operations teams stand ready to fight—any time, and anywhere.

The Fleet Antiterrorism Security Team (FAST) Company was established in 1987. This top U.S. special ops team is specially trained to quickly carry out dangerous missions around the world. FAST Company's motto is "Anytime, Anyplace."

Glossary

Allies (AL-lyz)—a group of countries united against Germany during World War II, including France, the United States, Canada, Great Britain, and others

ambush (AM-bush)—to hide and make a surprise attack

amphibious (am-FI-bee-uhs)—describes a military action involving forces landing and attacking from the sea

bombard (bom-BAHRD)—to attack a place with heavy gunfire

brigade (bri-GAYD)—a unit of an army, usually made up of two or more battalions

bunker (BUHNG-kuhr)—an underground shelter from bomb attacks and gunfire

casualty (KAZH-oo-uhl-tee)—people who are injured, captured, killed, or missing in a battle or war

Confederate (kuhn-FED-er-uht)—having to do with the Confederacy during the Civil War

D-Day (DEE-day)—June 6, 1944, the day that thousands of Allied forces began their invasion of France to free the country and the rest of Europe from the Germans during World War II

intelligence (in-TEL-uh-jenss)—secret information about an enemy's plans or actions

mercenary (MUR-suh-nayr-ee)—a soldier who is paid to fight for a foreign army

mortar (MOR-tur)—a short cannon that fires shells or rockets high in the air

perimeter (puh-RIM-uh-tur)—the outer edge or boundary of an area

stealth (STELTH)—the ability to move without being detected

Viet Cong (VEE-et KOHNG)—South Vietnamese rebel fighters who were aided by North Vietnam during the Vietnam War

Read More

Gordon, Nick. *Marine Corps Force Recon.* U.S. Military. Minneapolis: Bellwether Media, 2013.

Green, Michael. *The United States Marines.* U.S. Military Forces. Mankato, Minn.: Capstone Press, 2013.

Hamilton, John. *United States Marine Corps.* United States Armed Forces. Edina, Minn.: ABDO, 2012.

Internet Sites

FactHound offers a safe, fun way to find Internet sites related to this book. All of the sites on FactHound have been researched by our staff.

Here's all you do:

Visit *www.facthound.com*

Type in this code: 9781491487044

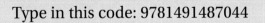

 Check out projects, games and lots more at
www.capstonekids.com

Critical Thinking Using the Common Core

1. How do you think that capturing important airfields on Pacific islands helped the U.S. war effort during World War II? (Key Ideas and Details)

2. Describe how gathering information about enemy forces can help special forces teams successfully achieve their missions. (Integration of Knowledge and Ideas)

Index